>YOU+DO-THE÷MATHS

Maths that's out of this world!

LAUNCH A ROCKET INTO SPACE

HILARY KOLL AND **STEVE MILLS**

ILLUSTRATED BY **VLADIMIR ALEKSIC**

QED Publishing

D0493629

Created for QED Publishing, Inc. by Tall Tree Ltd
Editor: Jon Richards
Designers: Ed Simkins and Jonathan Vipond
Illustrator: Vladimir Aleksic

QED Editorial Director: Victoria Garrard
QED Art Director: Laura Roberts-Jensen
QED Editor: Tasha Percy
QED Designer: Krina Patel

First published in the UK in 2014 by
QED Publishing
A Quarto Group company
The Old Brewery, 6 Blundell Street
London, N7 9BH

www.qed-publishing.co.uk

A catalogue record for this book is available from the British Library.

ISBN 978 1 78171 692 2

Printed in China

CONTENTS

Hi, my name is Michael and I'm an astronaut. I'm going to show you how maths can help you blast beyond Earth's atmosphere and into space! Are you ready?

Words in **bold** are explained in the glossary on page 32.

ASTRONAUT SELECTION

You have been chosen to lead a mission into space and your first task is to select astronauts for your team. Choosing astronauts for space missions is difficult. Applicants must have the correct qualifications and experience.

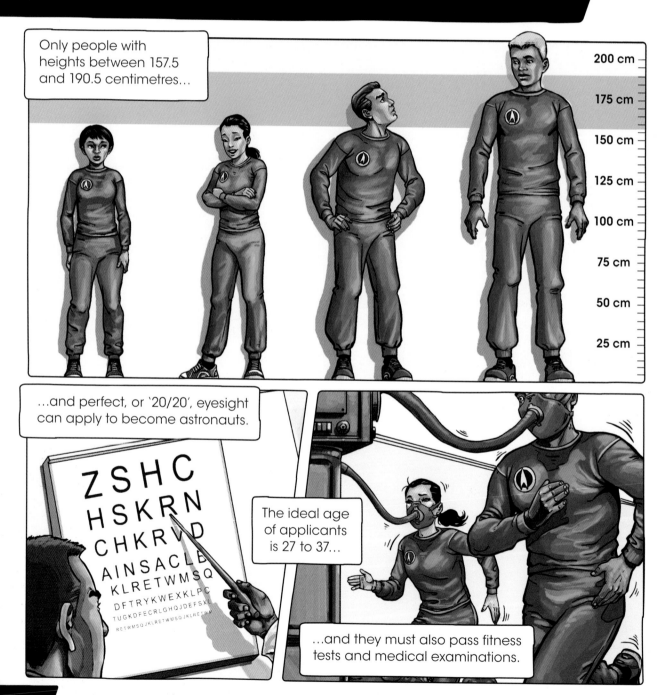

Only people with heights between 157.5 and 190.5 centimetres…

200 cm
175 cm
150 cm
125 cm
100 cm
75 cm
50 cm
25 cm

…and perfect, or '20/20', eyesight can apply to become astronauts.

The ideal age of applicants is 27 to 37…

…and they must also pass fitness tests and medical examinations.

This table shows nine people who would like to join your mission.

ASTRONAUT CANDIDATES

NAME	GENDER	AGE	HEIGHT	EYESIGHT	✓ ✗
Urvi Patel	Female	26	154.9 cm	20/20	
Brad Winchester	Male	30	157.3 cm	not 20/20	
Connor Wood	Male	28	177.0 cm	20/20	✗
Zoe Hurworth	Female	32	164.3 cm	20/20	
Samuel Wilkinson	Male	41	192.4 cm	20/20	
Kamelia Horacia	Female	37	166.2 cm	not 20/20	
Emily Smith	Female	39	158.1 cm	20/20	
Brendon Burke	Male	29	187.2 cm	20/20	
James Morton	Male	38	210.5 cm	20/20	

❶ How many of the candidates are within the preferred age range?

❷ Which of the candidates have the correct height to be an astronaut?

❸ Three of the candidates have the correct height, the preferred age and 20/20 eyesight. Who are they and are they male or female?

WHAT ABOUT THIS?
Find out your own height and see how much more you need to grow to be able to apply to be an astronaut. How much older do you need to be?

THE HISTORY OF ROCKETS

With your astronauts chosen, it's time to focus on the rocket.
But how much do you know about rockets?

This **timeline** shows some of the key events in the history of rockets.

Italian Claude Ruggieri launched animals inside rockets – the animals landed safely using parachutes.

A Sputnik rocket launched the first artificial satellite, *Sputnik 1*.

An Atlas rocket launched *Mariner 2*, the first spacecraft to reach another planet.

1806   1926   1957   1961 1963

Robert Goddard invented and launched the first liquid-fuelled rocket.

A Vostok-K rocket carried the first person into space, Russian cosmonaut Yuri Gagarin.

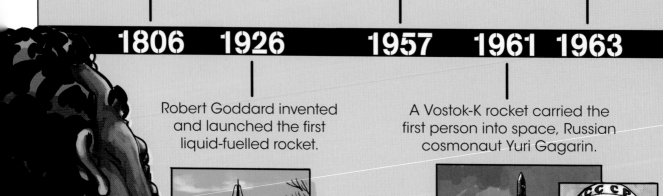

1. What happened 31 years before the year 2000?

2. Who invented and launched a rocket 70 years after 1856?

3. How many years after Apollo 11 landed on the Moon was the first Space Shuttle launched?

4. Which spacecraft reached another planet 41 years before SpaceShipOne reached space?

5. Which satellite went into space 56 years before the Olympic torch?

6. How long before the first Space Shuttle was launched was the first liquid-fuelled rocket launched?

The United States launched the first Space Shuttle, *Columbia*.

The Russian Soyuz rocket took the Olympic torch to the International Space Station.

1969   1981   2004   2013   NOW

A Saturn V rocket launched Apollo 11, which took the first people to the Moon.

SpaceShipOne became the first privately developed reusable rocket craft to reach space.

Your mission into space!

WHAT ABOUT THIS?
Choose four events from the timeline and work out how many years ago each happened.

ROCKET SHAPES

Your rocket will need to be streamlined. A streamlined vehicle can move through the air easily. Rockets must be streamlined so that they can reach speeds fast enough to take them into space.

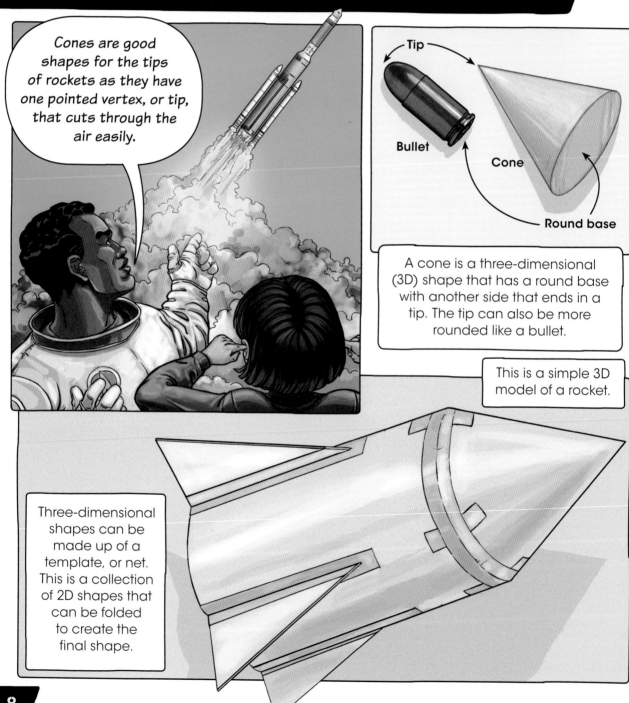

Cones are good shapes for the tips of rockets as they have one pointed vertex, or tip, that cuts through the air easily.

Tip

Bullet

Cone

Round base

A cone is a three-dimensional (3D) shape that has a round base with another side that ends in a tip. The tip can also be more rounded like a bullet.

This is a simple 3D model of a rocket.

Three-dimensional shapes can be made up of a template, or net. This is a collection of 2D shapes that can be folded to create the final shape.

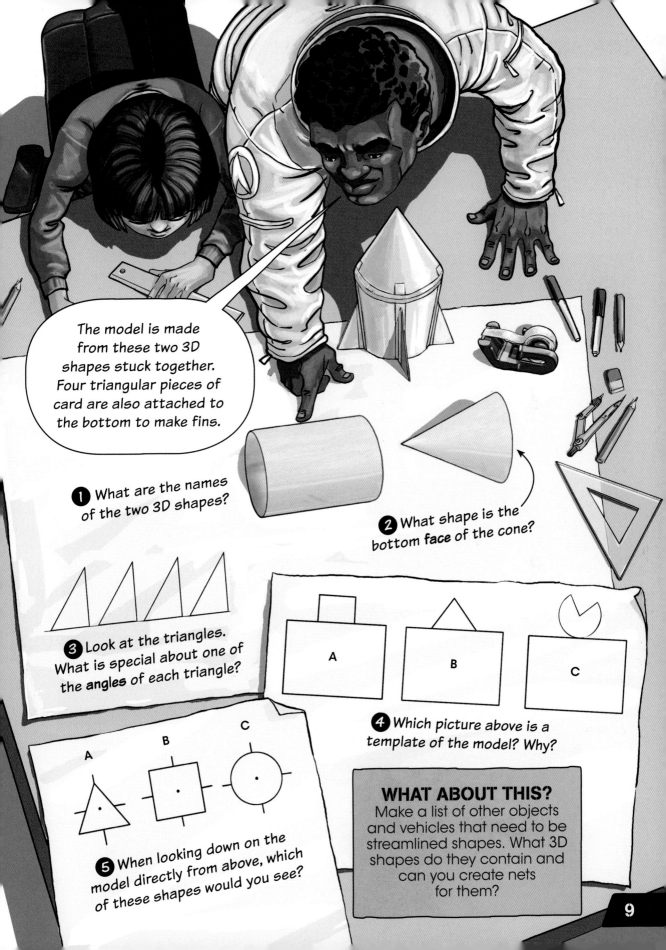

The model is made from these two 3D shapes stuck together. Four triangular pieces of card are also attached to the bottom to make fins.

1 What are the names of the two 3D shapes?

2 What shape is the bottom **face** of the cone?

3 Look at the triangles. What is special about one of the **angles** of each triangle?

4 Which picture above is a template of the model? Why?

A   B   C

A   B   C

5 When looking down on the model directly from above, which of these shapes would you see?

WHAT ABOUT THIS?
Make a list of other objects and vehicles that need to be streamlined shapes. What 3D shapes do they contain and can you create nets for them?

THE SIZE OF ROCKETS

Rockets that carry spacecraft or satellites into space have to be really large. This is to hold all the fuel needed. Your next job is to look at other rockets to see how big yours needs to be.

Did you know that a space rocket can be taller than a 30-storey building?

This table shows the heights of some famous buildings and rockets.

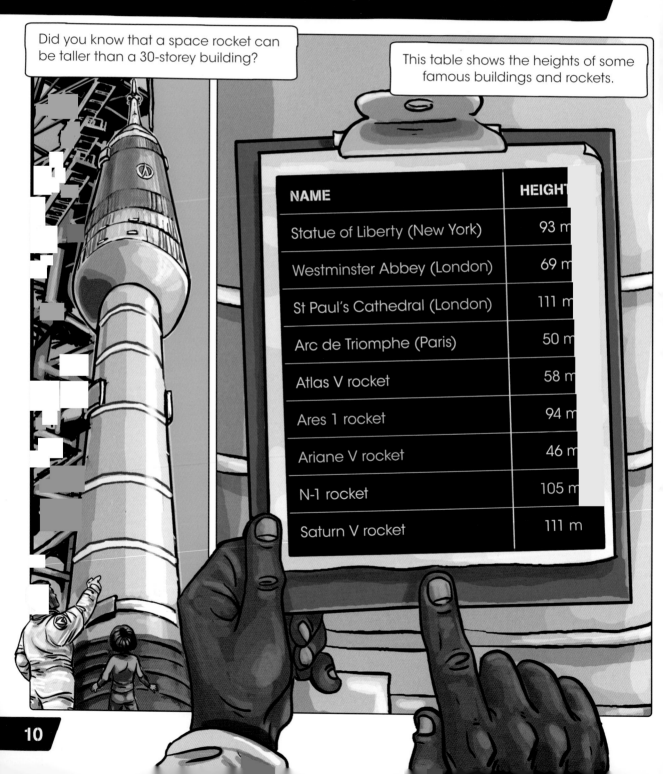

NAME	HEIGHT
Statue of Liberty (New York)	93 m
Westminster Abbey (London)	69 m
St Paul's Cathedral (London)	111 m
Arc de Triomphe (Paris)	50 m
Atlas V rocket	58 m
Ares 1 rocket	94 m
Ariane V rocket	46 m
N-1 rocket	105 m
Saturn V rocket	111 m

Atlas V rocket
58 m

Ares 1 rocket
94 m

Ariane V rocket
46 m

N-1 rocket
105 m

Saturn V rocket
111 m

❶ How much taller is:
a) the Atlas V rocket than the Arc de Triomphe?
b) the Ares 1 rocket than Westminster Abbey?
c) the Saturn V rocket than the Statue of Liberty?

❷ List the five rockets in order of height from shortest to tallest.

❸ Which rocket is:
a) the same height as St Paul's Cathedral?
b) 12 metres taller than the Statue of Liberty?
c) 23 metres shorter than Westminster Abbey?

❹ Round the height of each building and rocket to the nearest 10 metres.

WHAT ABOUT THIS?
Find out the height of other tall buildings in your country and see how much taller they are than the rockets listed here.

ROCKET CONSTRUCTION

A space rocket is built in several parts, called stages. Each stage has its own fuel and rocket engine. Your rocket will need three stages to carry it to outer space.

As the fuel in each stage is burnt up, the stage comes off and falls back to Earth.

Here, stages 1, 2 and 3 drop off leaving only the upper stage to travel into space.

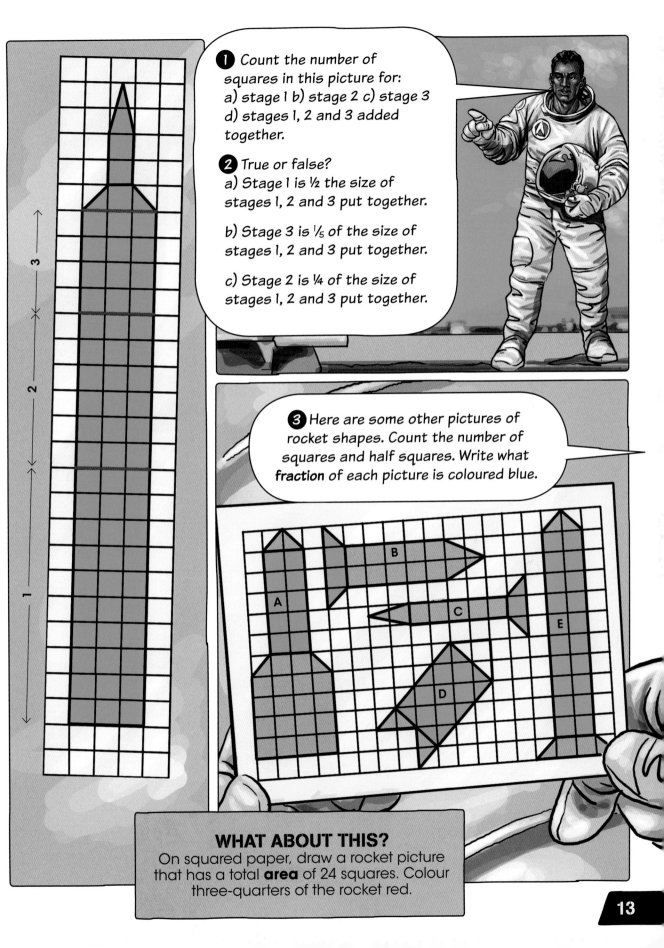

1 Count the number of squares in this picture for:
a) stage 1 b) stage 2 c) stage 3
d) stages 1, 2 and 3 added together.

2 True or false?
a) Stage 1 is ½ the size of stages 1, 2 and 3 put together.

b) Stage 3 is ⅕ of the size of stages 1, 2 and 3 put together.

c) Stage 2 is ¼ of the size of stages 1, 2 and 3 put together.

3 Here are some other pictures of rocket shapes. Count the number of squares and half squares. Write what **fraction** of each picture is coloured blue.

WHAT ABOUT THIS?
On squared paper, draw a rocket picture that has a total **area** of 24 squares. Colour three-quarters of the rocket red.

GETTING READY FOR LAUNCH

You can wear normal clothes inside the spacecraft as the air pressure is kept the same as on Earth.

If you go outside, however, you will have to wear a white pressurized space suit, as there is no air in space.

During launch, you will wear a special orange suit called an Advanced Crew Escape Suit, which will help protect you if there is an emergency.

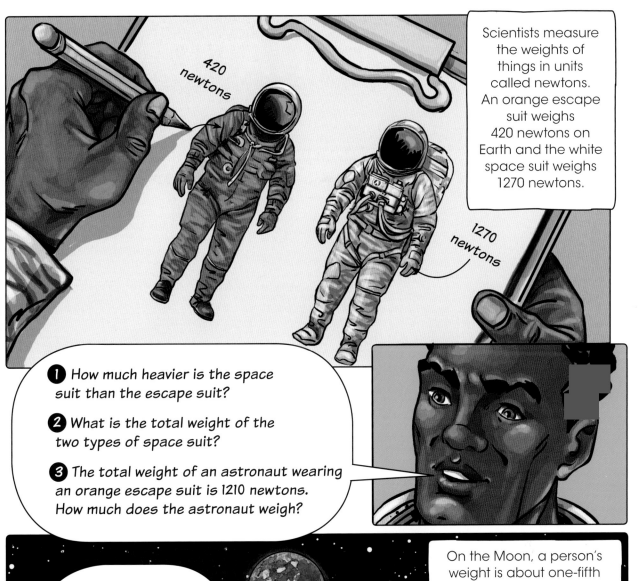

Scientists measure the weights of things in units called newtons. An orange escape suit weighs 420 newtons on Earth and the white space suit weighs 1270 newtons.

420 newtons

1270 newtons

1 How much heavier is the space suit than the escape suit?

2 What is the total weight of the two types of space suit?

3 The total weight of an astronaut wearing an orange escape suit is 1210 newtons. How much does the astronaut weigh?

On the Moon, a person's weight is about one-fifth of their weight on Earth.

4 What would each of these weigh on the Moon, if their weight on Earth is:

a) 2000 newtons?
b) 2050 newtons?
c) 1950 newtons?

WHAT ABOUT THIS?
Find out your own weight and work out about how much you would weigh on the Moon. What if you were wearing a space suit too?

FOOD PREPARATION

When you go into space, you will need to eat and drink, just like you do on Earth.

Sometimes, food is kept in small plastic packets to stop crumbs getting into electronics.

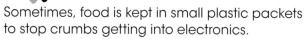

The energy that you get from food is measured in units called calories. Here is the calorie content for different types of food.

	FOOD	CALORIES
	1 egg	78
	1 tortilla (flat bread)	101
	1 cheese slice	69
	1 apple	84
	1 slice of pizza	237
	1 serving of mashed potato	214
	1 dried apricot	16
	1 floret of broccoli	11
	1 cooked chicken breast	358

Bread is not usually taken because without gravity the crumbs might float around and cause problems with the equipment. Tortillas are taken instead.

1 Work out the total number of calories for:

a) two eggs
b) a tortilla and an egg
c) five dried apricots
d) three apples
e) a chicken breast and a serving of mashed potato
f) four florets of broccoli
g) a slice of pizza with an extra cheese slice on top
h) three slices of pizza.

2 Work out which items from the list were eaten if an astronaut ate:

a) two items with a total of 248 calories
b) three items with a total of 583 calories
c) three items with a total of 254 calories.

WHAT ABOUT YOU?
If you had to eat between 1000 and 2000 calories per day, which of the items and how many of them would you eat?

COUNTDOWN!

All your preparations are complete, so it's time for the countdown to your mission to begin.

A countdown is a list of all the things that have to be done before a rocket is launched.

14:15
-1H 15M

It tells everyone, including the astronauts and the people in the control room, when each thing needs to be done.

Here is the countdown to your launch.

Step 1	-12 h 00 m 00 s	Final countdown begins
Step 2	-8 h 00 m 00 s	Check all electrics
Step 3	-1 h 30 m 00 s	Check launch system
Step 4	-8 m 00 s	Send 'All systems go' message
Step 5	-4 m 00 s	Pressurize tanks
Step 6	-1 m 00 s	Switch to onboard power mode
Step 7	-10 s	Begin 10 second countdown
Step 8	00 s	Ignite main engine and LAUNCH!

1 How many minutes before launch should:

a) the tanks be pressurized?
b) the launch system be checked?
c) all electrics be checked?

2 How many seconds before launch should:

a) the onboard power mode be switched on?
b) the tanks be pressurized?
c) the 'All systems go' message be sent?

3 If the launch is due to be at 15:30, what time should each step start?

10, 9, 8, 7, 6, 5, 4, 3, 2, 1...

BLAST OFF!

WHAT ABOUT THIS?
Choose a day, for example a Saturday. If the time you go to bed is at 00 seconds, write down five things you might do in the day and how long before bedtime, or 00 seconds, you might do them.

BLAST OFF!

With the countdown complete, your rocket blasts clear of the launchpad.

During the first part of the flight, your rocket goes straight up, vertically.

It then begins to lean, gradually, until it is at the best angle for building up speed and getting into orbit around the Earth.

INTO SPACE

As your rocket accelerates through the Earth's atmosphere, the temperature outside your spacecraft drops.

Space starts when you reach a height, or altitude, of 100 km above the Earth's surface.

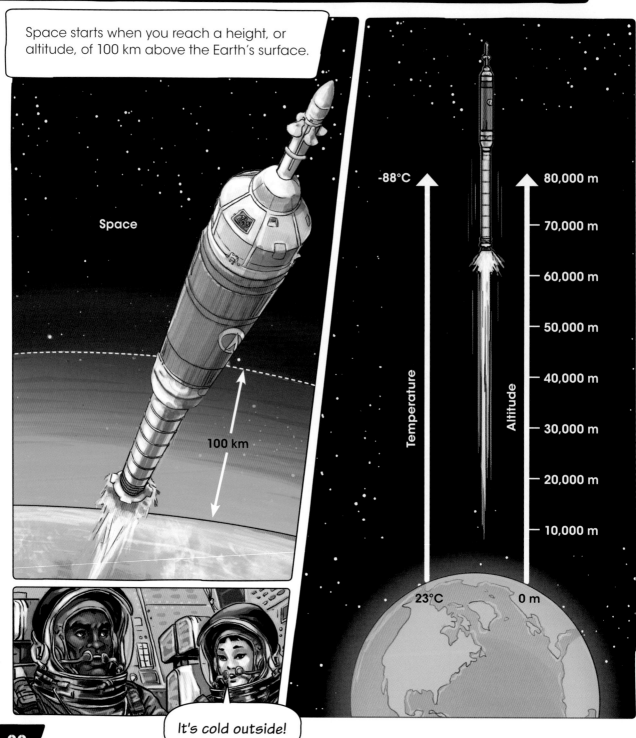

Space

100 km

-88°C

Temperature

Altitude

80,000 m

70,000 m

60,000 m

50,000 m

40,000 m

30,000 m

20,000 m

10,000 m

23°C

0 m

It's cold outside!

This table shows the altitude of the rocket and the temperature at that height.

Altitude	Temperature	Altitude	Temperature
0 m	23°C	4264 m	-17°C
980 m	9°C	5000 m	-20°C
1952 m	0°C	8054 m	-45°C
2172 m	-4°C	10,000 m	-60°C
3447 m	-10°C	80,000 m	-88°C

❶ How many kilometres above the Earth is the rocket when the temperature is:

a) –20°C?
b) –60°C?
c) –88°C?

❷ When the rocket is at these heights, what is the **difference** in temperatures?

a) 980 m and 0 m
b) 1952 m and 0 m
c) 2172 m and 1952 m
d) 8054 m and 1952 m
e) 2172 m and 4264 m
f) 10,000 m and 80,000 m.

❸ At what height is the rocket when it is 41 degrees colder than the temperature at 2172 m?

❹ At what height is the rocket when it is 54 degrees colder than its temperature at 980 m?

WHAT ABOUT THIS?
Check the weather forecast to see what the temperature will be tomorrow. How much warmer will it be than the temperature at an altitude of 80 kilometres?

23

IN THE COCKPIT

Sitting in the pilot's seat of your spacecraft, you'll face a control panel that has lots of scales, dials and readouts. These show information on how the rocket is performing.

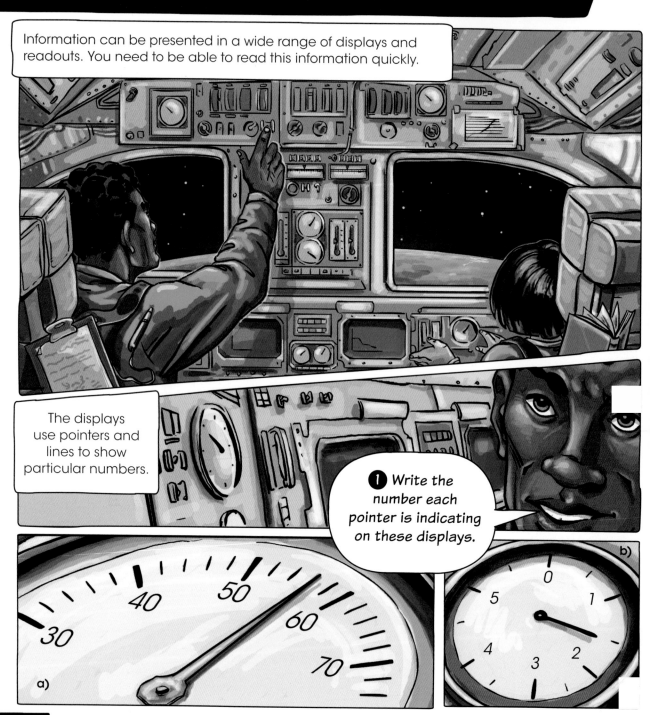

Information can be presented in a wide range of displays and readouts. You need to be able to read this information quickly.

The displays use pointers and lines to show particular numbers.

1 Write the number each pointer is indicating on these displays.

a)

b)

c)

d)

500
400   600
300   700
200   800
100   900
0   1000

2 Write the number each pointer is indicating on these scales below.

a)

300   400   500   600

b)

700   800   900   1000

c)

700 800 900 1000 1100 1200 1300 1400

d)

1700 1800 1900 2000 2100 2200 2300 2400

This display features a **line graph** showing the height above the Earth (altitude) against time from the launch.

Height above the Earth in km (Altitude)

100
90
80
70
60
50
40
30
20
10
0

0   1   2   3   4   5   6   7
Time from launch in minutes

3 Answer these questions about the graph.

a) How many kilometres above the Earth was the rocket after 5 minutes?
b) At what time was the rocket about 75 km above the Earth?

WHAT ABOUT THIS?
Write the names of five places where you might read a scale.

IN ORBIT

The rocket has done its job in launching your spacecraft into orbit around the Earth.

Your spacecraft orbits the Earth every 1½ hours.

Earth

1½ hours

During each orbit, you will have 45 minutes of daylight and then 45 minutes of darkness.

These clocks show some of the sunrise and sunset times.

1 Write each time in words.

a) Sunrise

b) Sunrise

c) Sunrise

d) Sunset

e) Sunset

f) Sunset

a) **01:40** Sunrise

b) **04:10** Sunrise

c) **02:25** Sunset

d) **04:55** Sunset

2 Write the above times using the words 'past' and 'to'.

Use a **24-hour clock** to answer these questions.

3 If the Sun rises at 11:40, write the times of the next three sunrises the astronauts will see.

4 If the Sun sets at 19:25, write the times of the next three sunsets the astronauts will see.

WHAT ABOUT THIS?
Read what time it is now on a clock.
What's the time in 45 minutes? Keep counting on in intervals of 45 minutes. Will you reach the same time 24 hours later or not?

RETURN TO EARTH

With your mission complete, your spacecraft can return to Earth. It has to re-enter the atmosphere before landing.

First, your spacecraft fires small rockets to slow down and turn around so that it descends bottom-first.

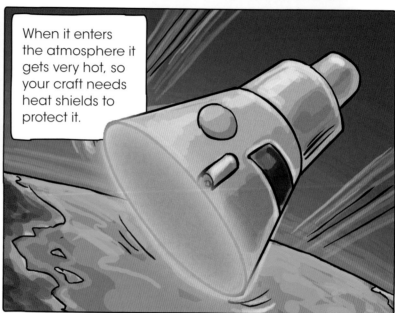

When it enters the atmosphere it gets very hot, so your craft needs heat shields to protect it.

As it gets closer to the ground, it slows down by making S-shaped turns, using parachutes, or by firing more rockets until it can land safely.

1 Describe the series of turns shown in these pictures, using the words 'quarter turn', 'half turn', 'clockwise' and 'anticlockwise'.

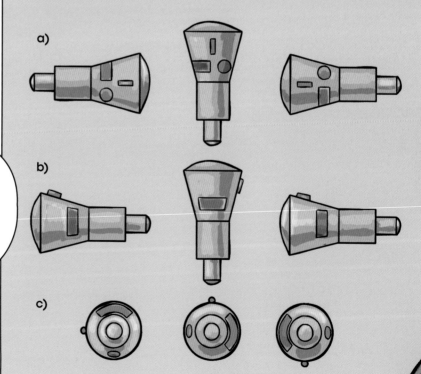

a)

b)

c)

28

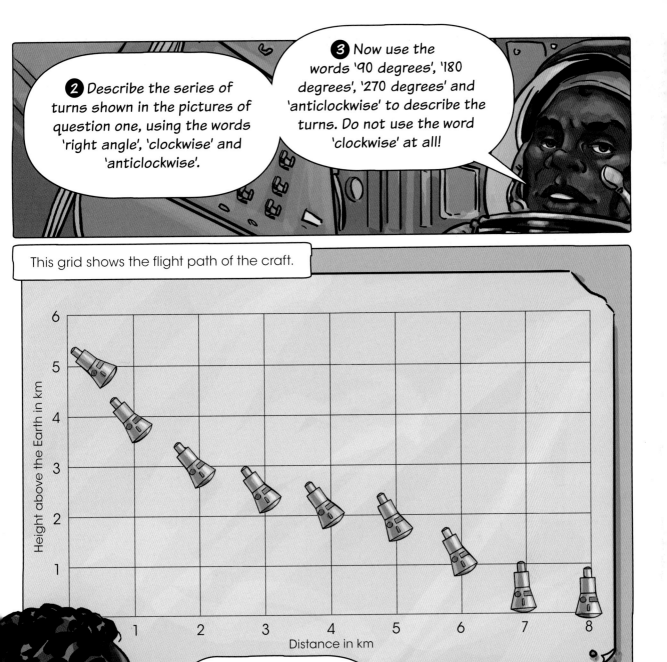

2 Describe the series of turns shown in the pictures of question one, using the words 'right angle', 'clockwise' and 'anticlockwise'.

3 Now use the words '90 degrees', '180 degrees', '270 degrees' and 'anticlockwise' to describe the turns. Do not use the word 'clockwise' at all!

This grid shows the flight path of the craft.

4 Write 'yes' or 'no' to show whether the craft crossed the points:

a) (2, 3)
b) (1, 6)
c) (2, 5)
d) (5, 2).

WHAT ABOUT THIS?
Cut out a small rocket shape from a sheet of card. Put it on the centre of a circular protractor. Turn the rocket and work out how many degrees it has rotated.

ANSWERS

Congratulations! You have completed your space mission! Check your answers here and see how well you did.

PAGES 4–5

1. Five

2. Connor, Zoe, Kamelia, Emily and Brendon

3. Connor, Zoe and Brendon (male, female and male)

PAGES 6–7

1. A Saturn V rocket launched Apollo 11.

2. Robert Goddard

3. 12 years

4. Mariner 2

5. Sputnik 1

6. 55 years

PAGES 8–9

1. Cone and tube (or cylinder)

2. Circle

3. One angle is a right angle.

4. C. The top part rolls up to make the cone.

5. C

PAGES 10–11

1. a) 8 metres b) 25 metres c) 18 metres

2. Ariane V, Atlas V, Ares 1, N-1, Saturn V

3. a) Saturn V b) N-1 c) Ariane V

4.

NAME	HEIGHT
Statue of Liberty (New York)	90 m
Westminster Abbey (London)	70 m
St Paul's Cathedral (London)	110 m
Arc de Triomphe (Paris)	50 m
Atlas V rocket	60 m
Ares 1 rocket	90 m
Ariane V rocket	50 m
N-1 rocket	110 m
Saturn V rocket	110 m

PAGES 12–13

1. a) 30 b) 18 c) 12 d) 60

2. a) true b) true c) false, it is $^3/_5$

3. a) 10 out of 30 squares = $^1/_3$
   b) 3 out of 15 squares = $^1/_5$
   c) 2 out of 8 squares = $^1/_4$
   d) 12 out of 14 squares = $^6/_7$
   e) 20 out of 24 squares = $^5/_6$

PAGES 14–15

1. 850 newtons

2. 1690 newtons

3. 790 newtons

4. a) 400 newtons b) 410 newtons
   c) 390 newtons

PAGES 16–17

1. a) 156 calories   b) 179 calories,
   c) 80 calories   d) 252 calories,
   e) 572 calories   f) 44 calories,
   g) 306 calories   h) 711 calories

2. a) one slice of pizza and one floret
   of broccoli
   b) one chicken breast, one serving of
   mashed potato and one floret of
   broccoli
   c) one tortilla, one cheese slice and
   one apple

PAGES 18–19

1. a) 4 minutes b) 90 minutes
   c) 480 minutes

2. a) 60 seconds b) 240 seconds
   c) 480 seconds

3. Step 1 03:30, Step 2 07:30, Step 3 14:00,
   Step 4 15:22, Step 5 15:26, Step 6 15:29,
   Step 7 15:29 and 50 seconds

PAGES 20–21

1. a) 90° b) yes

2. 70°

3. Step 3 – 30°, Step 4 – 45°, Step 5 – 60°

4. Step 4

5. acute

6. 30°

WHAT ABOUT THIS? 7° per minute

PAGES 22–23

1. a) 5 km b) 10 km c) 80 km

2. a) 14°C b) 23°C c) 4°C d) 45°C e) 13°C
   f) 28°C

3. 8054 m

4. 8054 m

PAGES 24–25

1. a) 56 b) 1½ or 1.5 c) –2 d) 750

2. a) 440 b) 840 c) 1060 d) 2040

3. a) about 50 km b) about 6 minutes

PAGES 26–27

1. a) ten past six   b) twenty to nine
   c) ten past eleven   d) five to seven
   e) twenty-five past nine   f) five to twelve

2. a) twenty to two b) ten past four
   c) twenty-five past two d) five to five

3. 13:10, 14:40, 16:10

4. 20:55, 22:25, 23:55

PAGES 28–29

1. a) quarter turn anticlockwise and then
   another quarter turn anticlockwise
   b) quarter turn clockwise and then a quarter
   turn anticlockwise
   c) quarter turn clockwise and then a half
   turn (either clockwise or anticlockwise)

2. a) a right angle anticlockwise and then
   another right angle anticlockwise
   b) right angle clockwise and then a right
   angle anticlockwise
   c) a right angle clockwise and then two right
   angles (either clockwise or anticlockwise)

3. a) 90° anticlockwise and then 90°
   anticlockwise
   b) 270° anticlockwise and then 90°
   anticlockwise
   c) 270° anticlockwise and then 180°
   anticlockwise

4. a) yes b) no c) no d) yes

GLOSSARY

24-HOUR CLOCK
A clock that uses the numbers 0 to 23 to show the hours of a day. Midnight is 00:00 and midday is 12:00.

ACUTE
An angle that is less than 90 degrees.

ANGLE
An angle is an amount of turn. It is measured in degrees, such as 90°, which is also known as a right angle.

AREA
The amount of surface a shape covers.

DIFFERENCE
The difference between two numbers can be found by subtracting the smaller number from the larger one.

FACE
A surface of a 3D shape. For example, a cube has six square-shaped faces.

FRACTION
A part of a whole. The number on the bottom of the fraction (the denominator) tells you how many equal parts the whole has been split into. The number on the top (the numerator) tells you the number of equal parts being described.

HORIZONTAL
Straight across.

LINE GRAPH
A line graph shows information by using points and lines on a grid. Line graphs are often used to show changes over time.

OBTUSE
An angle that is greater than 90 degrees.

PERPENDICULAR
When an object or a line is at right angles to another object or line.

REFLEX
An angle that is greater than 180 degrees.

ROUND
To round a number to the nearest 10 means to say which multiple of 10 it is closest to.

TIMELINE
A line that shows events in chronological (date) order.

VERTICAL
Straight up.

INDEX